LIVING IN A
FRAGILE WORLD

Text and cover illustration copyright © Peter Privett 2003
Inside illustrations copyright © Mary Hall 2003
The author asserts the moral right
to be identified as the author of this work

Published by
The Bible Reading Fellowship
First Floor, Elsfield Hall
15–17 Elsfield Way, Oxford OX2 8FG

ISBN 1 84101 325 0
First published 2003
10 9 8 7 6 5 4 3 2 1 0

Acknowledgments
Unless otherwise stated, scripture quotations are taken from the Contemporary English Version of the
Bible published by HarperCollins Publishers, copyright © 1991, 1992, 1995 American Bible Society.

Performance and copyright
The right to present *Things that go bump in the night* Godly Play material is included in the purchase
price, so long as the presentation is in an amateur context, for instance in church services, schools or
holiday club venues. Where any charge is made to participants, written permission must be obtained
from the author, who can be contacted through the publishers. A fee or royalties may be payable for the
right to present the material in that context.

A catalogue record for this book is available from the British Library

Printed and bound in Malta

LIVING IN A FRAGILE WORLD

A SPIRITUAL EXPLORATION OF CONSERVATION AND CITIZENSHIP
USING THE METHODS OF GODLY PLAY

PETER PRIVETT

WHAT IS GODLY PLAY?

Godly Play is a method of Christian education and spiritual direction, which uses religious language and symbol to help people become more aware of the mystery of God's presence in their lives.

- Stories and material are offered in an open way.
- People are encouraged to enter into the stories, language and symbols.
- Space is created to relate these to life and experience.

The heart of Godly Play

Godly Play uses liturgical action and ritual to make meaning by:

- Creating sacred space
- Building and working in community
- Learning religious language

What happens in a Godly Play session?

In a *Godly Play* session people are invited into a space to experience a sacred story, a parable or liturgical action. As well as words, objects and symbols are used to give a visual focus and tap into other ways of knowing. Open questions follow, giving people an opportunity to explore and deepen the meanings of the story… to play with the possibilities.

This is followed by individual free work which might include using the physical objects / symbols, using silence, using writing materials or some basic art materials.

There is a free choice of activity designed to encourage further playing in the presence of God. A time of feasting and sharing closes the session.

Living in a fragile world draws on some of the elements of this methodology, although the sessions do not always contain the elements of a customary Godly Play session.

CONTENTS

Foreword 6

PART ONE: PREPARATION   7

A story for the night...8
Introduction..11
Outline of the sessions...15
Materials and patterns 18

PART TWO: LIVING IN A FRAGILE WORLD   25

Session One 26
Session Two 32
Session Three 40
Session Four 46
Session Five 51
Appendix One: Templates 57
Appendix Two: Additional exercises 63

FOREWORD

The bigger the problem or challenge, the more vital it is to use imagination and creativity. Worthy reports, intellectual debate and token gestures too often fail to help communities to engage at a deep enough level with conservation and citizenship issues. This book is a unique guide to exploring our relationship to the world, its resources and each other in the deepest and widest sense—as spiritual issues.

Living in a fragile world brilliantly combines both the *content* for framing a spiritual perspective on environmental matters and a thoroughly imaginative and spiritual *process* to support the sessions. This integrity of content and method is rare. Be warned, it's also deeply powerful and transformative. If you just want your group to think with their heads about how to live carefully in the world, this book isn't for you. This course of sessions gets to the heart and soul of the matter, and treats the participants as having hearts and souls too. It's teaching, but not as we've known it!

When Peter Privett applies his imagination and creative talents as an educator, *Godly Play* trainer and teaching consultant, it's easy to feel inadequate. He seems to ooze innovative, playful, thought-provoking ways of doing everything—colleagues, like me, are very jealous! But the beauty of this book is that it shares all this talent with more normal mortals.

One of the book's key strengths as a practical guide to working much more creatively and spiritually is that everything in these pages is the result of careful piloting with children and adults alike. The process and content of these sessions will really work. And yet there nothing to prescribe the direction *your* group will necessarily take and no manipulation of what they ought to end up thinking or feeling. Children, adults, leaders and participants will find in this all the structure they need to reach genuinely liberating insights and inspiration.

I wholeheartedly recommend this course and the approach to spiritual nurture it represents. You'll find it's lucidly written and has comprehensive, sensitive advice that both experienced and novice group leaders will find helpful. Its unusual to find a book marketed at children and adults, but perhaps this is an important part of why a spiritual approach to these issues is ultimately necessary for real understanding and commitment to change. George Eliot suggested, 'We could never have loved the earth so well if we had no childhood in it.' This book is a way for people of any age to tap into their childhood resources—qualities of wonder, playfulness, mystery and hopefulness—and find for themselves that often-mislaid love for the earth and all creation.

Dr Rebecca Nye, University of Cambridge

PART ONE

PREPARATION

A STORY FOR THE NIGHT

Imagine a group of people, gathered together in the depths of rural England for a series of evening meetings in the dark nights of March. The setting is an old rural church that has been rearranged with carpet and movable chairs to serve as both local place of worship and community hall. They've come together to explore the things that jar and jolt our contemporary experience, the things that make us sit up and question as we live in the ever-increasing fragility of this world.

The storyteller / leader sits quietly on the floor and, when all have assembled into a circle, gently starts to unroll a large piece of black velvet. A beautiful wooden box is then opened and star sequins are scattered over the cloth. 'I wonder if you have ever looked at the night sky, and seen how vast and immense it is… Have you ever wondered how far it stretches…?'

A small outline figure of a person is placed in the centre. 'Have you ever imagined how vast the universe is and thought of how small you are, but that you are part of this great universe…?'

The storyteller then takes one of the sequins, slowly brings it to the figure of the person and places it carefully on the heart, with the words, '…and that the universe is also part of you?'

A silence follows and it is obvious that people are caught up in the mystery and awe of creation, in the interconnectedness of things.

The rest of the velvet is unrolled to reveal a large blue circle representing planet earth, the landmasses of the continents are laid down, and time is given to enjoy and delight in the wonder of creation.

Then, 'things go bump in the night' boxes or bags are laid down, which eventually reveal some of the destructive forces at work on our planet—the forces that put increasing pressure upon the ever-increasing vulnerability of our world.

By the end of the process, something that was once beautiful now looks a mess.

A silence follows, and the leader asks some open-ended questions to enable the participants to give voice to some of their feelings and thoughts, perhaps to suggest some possible actions to recover the balance and connectedness of creation.

The session ends with a long period of silence, with a request that lights be shut off and candles lit.

Finally, the material is gathered away and tidied up by the group, with a suggestion that they think of what they might really do.

Two people are seen on their hands and knees, gathering the sequins back into the box.

One turns to the other and says, 'Look, I've got the stars of the universe in my hands… I never thought I'd be holding the stars of the universe in my hands.'

Each week, they return for a similar pattern.

Each week, the viewpoint hones closer and closer in.

Each week, the move is from the wider planetary view to the land, to the community, to the self.

Each week, the group is invited to recapture the interconnectedness of all things, to recapture something of the vision of God.

IN THE BEGINNING

The invitation and suggestion to explore this theme came from the Reverend Sylvia Turner, the vicar of a rural group of parishes in the Diocese of Hereford. During Lent, she wanted an opportunity for people to grapple with some important issues, not just giving up chocolate! Her concern for the environment, and the ever-increasing fragility of the earth, were at the heart of the matter. How can we become more aware of the complexity of interrelated issues? What actions might we have to take to effect changes? How can we relate to the resources of the earth and to each other in a more sustainable and relational way?

Set alongside this was a children's book called *The Boy and the Cloth of Dreams*. The story tells of a young boy who has been given a beautiful patchwork bedspread made by his grandmother. The cloth protects him from all his evil nightmares—until, one day, as he is carrying it around, he trips and rips it. During the evening, for the first time in his life he is confronted with fear and nightmare dreams. Through the torn cloth pour all the evil things that have been suppressed and kept at bay. The story continues to tell how the boy has to confront the evil, take action and eventually repair the dream cloth.

The juxtaposition of these elements gave birth to the title *Living in a fragile world*. When we as a human race—through neglect, accident and sometimes deliberate action—rip the fabric of the earth, how do we confront this evil, take action and bring about some form of restoration?

LIVING IN A FRAGILE WORLD

Who is it for?

Although this material is published as a children's resource, experience has shown that it can be used with adults and children alike, so I have tried to be inclusive.

As the storyteller, you are encouraged to adapt and change things to suit your particular situation—you must feel comfortable inside yourself with the material you are presenting. In one or two places, the imagery is sensitive, but don't automatically assume that the children won't cope. The hardest images in this material actually came from children themselves. It will all depend on the quality of relationships that you have in your group.

Why do it this way?

Martin Ashley has written of the importance of recovering a spiritual dimension in the area of environmental education. His research in the world of school education suggests that awareness and understanding are not sufficient to effect behavioural change. What is needed is a movement away from seeing the environment as another commodity, an object to be manipulated and a place where humans set themselves over and against it. He calls for a spiritual understanding, which includes an understanding of interconnectedness, of feelings of oneness with the ultimate, of the reintegration of subject and object. This spiritual dimension offers the possibility of integration between deeply held values, belief and behaviour. Ashley's research suggests that when these two dimensions are separated, then people will speak about their concern for the environment but in their actions they will do little, or even the opposite of what they say.

The apostle Paul also had a glimpse of this dilemma: 'I know that my selfish desires won't let me do anything that is good. Even when I want to do right, I cannot. Instead of doing what I know is right, I do wrong' (Romans 7:18–19).

For Paul, it all seems hopeless until we move to his next chapter. Chapter 8 of Paul's letter to the church at Rome contains his wonderful vision of the wholeness of creation, the groaning of creation as it works towards integration, the integration of flesh and spirit, the integration of struggle and achievement, the integration of death and life culminating in the person of Christ.

Ashley also hints at this:

The spiritually developed person is able to perceive meaning and purpose in life, as well as a mission or sense of purposeful vocation. He or she feels that all life is sacred and experiences feelings of wonder and awe which allow the perception of life as 'holy' (whether or not this is conceived in a religious sense). The spiritual person can appreciate material things but finds their contentment in non-material things and does not suffer a craving for possessions. He or she has a strong sense of social justice and is a visionary committed to a better world. Whilst possessed of a deep awareness of pain, suffering and the tragic, the spiritual person has come to terms with this aspect of reality and finds in it an enhancement of joy, appreciation and the value of life. This has discernible effect upon the person's relationship to self, others, nature, life and whatever one considers to be the ultimate.[1]

Ashley points to the work of David Hay and Rebecca Nye,[2] which suggests that young children often possess the above qualities naturally, but are then socially educated and conditioned out of them and into a consumerist approach. As adults, we may have to relearn or recover these qualities.

Jesus said, 'I promise you that you cannot get into God's kingdom, unless you accept it the way a child does' (Mark 10:15). This would seem to suggest that any education that wishes to explore a spiritual dimension must have at its heart the qualities, the essence, of childhood.

Living in a fragile world invites people to recover some of these childhood qualities and to engage with the story of our environment. It also invites us to play with the some of the possibilities of that story.

Those familiar with the work of Jerome Berryman and Godly Play[3] will see the direct influence of that work in this book, and I would like to acknowledge how deeply indebted I am to Jerome for introducing the experience of Godly Play to me. It feels very much like a home-coming, confirming a practice that feels familiar and true.

Godly Play is a well-tested method of working with children and is a means of experiencing and engaging with biblical, theological and liturgical material. It is a creative and imaginative religious education programme, and experience has proved that both young people and adults of all ages respond enthusiastically to this approach. A key feature of a Godly Play session is a story told carefully and respectfully, using models, figures, and visual aids.[4]

During a Godly Play session, the story is followed by a series of open-ended questions that invite the partici-pants to engage at another level, a level that puts the story alongside their experience. This is then followed by some creative activity, which is freely chosen by the participants and is an opportunity to meditate and reflect further upon the implications of the experience. The session ends with an opportunity for prayer and the sharing of simple food and drink. The pattern has a sacramental theme running right through it. Ordinary objects take on symbolic and representational meanings, and the non-verbal messages are as important as the verbal.

Living in a fragile world draws on some of the elements of this methodology, although the sessions do not always contain the elements of a customary Godly Play session.

Living in a fragile world will not answer the world's environmental problems. You may find that you don't like parts of the scripts. Some of the sessions might not be relevant to your situation. That's fine. Please feel free to experiment, alter things, and create your own versions. What I offer here is a starting point and an experience of what worked in one small part of the world. John Hull, the Professor of Religious Education at Birmingham University, has written extensively about his experience of blindness and, in several public lectures, has commented that this has taught him the importance of taking 'one small step at a time'.

Living in a fragile world is offered in the same vein. In a highly complex field with numerous voices claiming the stage, and a range of groups competing for the resources of the world, this book is offered as one very small step.

Notes

1. Martin Ashley, 'Behaviour change and environmental citizenship: a case for spiritual development?' in the *International Journal of Children's Spirituality*, Vol. 5 No. 2, Carfax Publishing Taylor and Francis Ltd, 2000, p. 141.
2. David Hay and Rebecca Nye, *The Spirit of the Child*, HarperCollins, 1998.
3. Jerome Berryman, *The Complete Guide to Godly Play* (4 volumes), The Living Word Press, 2002.
4. Sandra Pollerman, in her book, *Stories, stories everywhere* (BRF, 2001), outlines the importance and power of storytelling and also acknowledges the influences of Godly Play on her work as a storyteller.

INTRODUCTION

One of the biggest problems with environmental issues and, in fact, the whole area of spirituality is the ever-increasing privatization of everything. What we need to recover is a sense of community working, community values, and community solutions. We will never do it on our own.

One of the beneficial effects of sharing a story is that, when it works well, it creates community. It creates a shared experience. The open reflection of that story can then create a community response and shared action.

A SAFE PLACE TO EXPLORE

Sometimes groups can be creative and exciting places of learning, and sometimes the opposite happens. Most people learn well when there are feelings of trust and security established in the group.

Within the groups that you bring together, each person needs to know and feel that his or her opinions and words are valued and important. Before you begin your group sessions, you may find that you will have to set aside some time to agree some simple group rules.

The following suggestions may help you to start. You could write them up on flip-chart paper or make individual copies. You may want to order them differently, express them in your own words, or illustrate them with cartoons or images.

- People speak for themselves—'I think... I feel'—instead of speaking for others.
- People are allowed to speak without being interrupted or cut across.
- People are able to ask for clarification or explanation.
- People who take some time to give voice to their thoughts are given space to think first, then speak.
- People who find it easy to talk are given time to be silent so that others can speak.
- People's opinions are respected in this group. (It may be necessary to have some discussion outside the group time about what can or cannot be said or shared.)
- People keep focused on the subject / task.
- People try to be of service to others in the group.

There may be other suggestions that the group feels are important.

THE STORYTELLER / LEADER

If the experience is to be one that involves community, the task of the leader is to guide and gently lead the other members through the process. You are not expected to know the right answers, or know the solutions to the problems. What a relief! Another relief is that the storyteller / leader doesn't have to be same person each time, so one person doesn't need to learn all the scripts. Share the stories among others so that different people have a turn at leading.

The task of the storyteller / leader is to present the story, ask some open-ended questions and trust the process, then sit back and discover with the others the truths that will be revealed. These truths cannot be pre-planned. They will arise during the course of the process. A key feature of this method is a *trust* that the group will discover its own learning, whether the participants are children, teenagers or adults.

Therefore, one of the key skills that the storyteller / leader needs is that of trust. One of the features of the Godly Play style of storytelling is that of restraint. As a former primary school teacher, I was very used to throwing the whole of myself into the story—acting it out with loud voices and large, dramatic gestures, and generally working the class or school into a frenzied response. I have similar memories from being a priest during the traditional family service.

The Godly Play style does the opposite. If the whole point is the creation of community, then the storyteller needs to disappear into the story so that the participants focus on the material and not the storyteller.

The storyteller / leader will need to read through the scripts first, and then practise the various movements with the objects and materials. Feel free to alter words and actions so that you feel comfortable with them. The words and actions you use need to be yours. The instructions and aids are there to start you off. As you practise the words and actions, you may discover that new possibilities arise, so go with them and make them your own.

One of the advantages of using objects and cloths is that they act as memory aids for the words. If possible, do not have the script by your side when you tell the story, as it can be very distracting. However, if you've never done it before and you're nervous, some key words on small cards might be helpful.

When it comes to the storytelling session itself, make sure you are there well before everyone else. Have all the props in place next to you or nearby. You may want to have the rolled black velvet cloth already in the circle. This has the advantage of creating a sense of expectancy. If you are in place as people arrive, again this creates a sense of drama and anticipation.

People may ask you what is going to happen. Try not to give away too much. Engage in conversation that plays with the expectations.

Some helpful techniques for storytelling

- Don't start the story until you are ready. Don't be pressurized into beginning. It's helpful to sit quietly, take some simple breaths, and then begin.
- Slow down the pace—silence sometimes speaks louder. It also gives the participants time to appreciate the different parts of the tale.
- Keep the volume gentle but audible. This aids concentration, and sets a meditative, reflective style.
- When handling the materials and visual aids, hold and move them with love and respect. Sometimes, the movement and actions are more powerful without words.
- Don't look at your audience; keep your eyes down on the material at all times. This is the hardest thing of

all, especially for schoolteachers working with children. Nevertheless, experience has shown, in this setting, that lack of eye contact has a dramatic effect on keeping your audience's attention. It seems to signal to the participants that something important is happening here. It draws them into the story. The simple rule seems to be that if you are in the story, then others are there as well.

I was recently telling stories in another context using this technique when there were several interruptions into the room and, finally, the ultimate distraction of the mobile phone. I decided to lower my voice and not look up. When debriefing the session, I found that none of the participants had been aware of the distractions. Experience has also shown that this technique works with all ages. Try it and see!

- When you have finished telling the story, sit back and create some silence before you lead into the questioning.

WONDERING QUESTIONS

This part of the session signals a change of mood. After the telling of the story, lead into a period of group reflection. Eye contact may well be appropriate at this point. The aim of this part of the session is to allow the group to verbalize and play with the possibilities.

The task of the leader here is to enable that open process to happen. It may be that someone different will lead this part of the session. Whoever it is, the reflection needs to be handled with sensitivity and care.

This is where the group rules of agreement need to be remembered. It may not be necessary to repeat them verbally, but whoever is leading needs to have them at the back of his or her mind. The leader of this part needs to be aware of their own views and feelings and be careful not to let them intrude. The task is to enable other members of the group to articulate their thoughts. In a Godly Play session, this part is called the 'wondering'.

Ask questions beginning with the words, 'I wonder': '*I wonder* which part of the story you liked best'… '*I wonder* which is the most important part of the story'… and so on.

The whole point of open questions is to enable people to express for themselves what the experience has been about and what possible insights and learning they have had. One aspect of this is that you cannot predict what the outcome will be. It will be dependent upon the time and place in which it happens. The Spirit will dictate, and will not be constrained by human control.

A key feature here is the same as in the storytelling experience—*trust*. One of the great fears that adults have in this setting stems from their educational experience, which has taught them that there are right and wrong answers to questions. Of course there are to some questions, but not all. In your 'wondering' session, there are no right or wrong answers. Adults often have a loud voice in them saying, 'Will I look foolish by saying the wrong thing?' This is why it is important to create an atmosphere of trust and security throughout the whole of the process. Generally speaking, children don't have as many fears as adults, although they may know intuitively the settings in which there might be right and wrong answers, and whom or whom not to trust. Teenagers often find group discussions difficult where they feel awkward and embarrassed.

One of the good things about the Godly Play process is that when the safe and secure place has been created, all three groups—children, teenagers and adults—respond openly and creatively. Another helpful thing is that the open questions focus on some specific aspects of the experience of the story, the experience of the last fifteen minutes or so. They focus, therefore, on something concrete and practical. People are not asked to offer their ideas on abstract theories outside their experience.

Each session outlined in this book has a set of open questions to ask. You may want to ask some more.

• Ask questions that have a wide variety of response.
• Ask questions that have responses other than 'Yes' or 'No'.
• Ask questions that begin with some general points, then move to specifics.
• Ask questions that allow people to become involved.
• Ask questions that explore some difficult aspects as well those that are comfortable. For example, 'I wonder which part of this story you didn't like, or would like to leave out.'

The task of this part of the session is to allow the group to go where it will, to make reflections, associations and connections.

Sometimes it is helpful, as the leader, to repeat what people have said, to show that it has been heard. In larger gatherings, it is helpful to relay the learning so that everybody can hear. This also provides an opportunity to affirm what has been said. If you don't understand or hear, then ask people to repeat what they have said.

Sometimes when the leader asks the first question, there is a silence and nobody responds. This is especially true in adult settings. Leave a space, and count to seven. It may be that people need some time to feel comfortable, or they may need some time to think through the question. Sometimes it is helpful, after the silence, to repeat the same question. People then receive permission to speak again. Inwardly, you may think that nothing is going to happen, and anxiety and panic rise within you, but learn to trust the silences. Be aware of your body language, and relax.

If nobody responds, go to the next question. This usually breaks the spell. For those of you who are pessimists—I know what you are thinking. 'What if no one responds to anything?' Don't ask that question! It will get you nowhere. Remember: *trust* the process and 'nowhere' becomes 'now here'.

Try to make sure that everybody has an opportunity to speak: be aware of the different members of the group. You can usually tell which people need longer to think things through before they speak and which members of the group are not speaking because they feel hurt and disengaged. Be aware of the body language of members of the group.

At some point, you may need to check whether those who haven't spoken want to contribute.

When people make contributions to the group, they may refer to different aspects of the story. It sometimes helps if you silently re-enact this part of the story using the figures, or point to the visual aid, or take it gently and hold it in your hand, while the person is speaking. This is a non-verbal signal that you are listening and have heard their comment. It can be a very powerful way of affirming the person.

It may be possible, in this section of the process, to rearrange some of the visual aids. Sometimes, turning something on its head, looking at it from an opposite viewpoint, helps us understand the issues more clearly. Therefore, some people may want to replay some parts of the story in a different way and explore other outcomes. If this happens, then rejoice and go with the flow. Experience has shown that really exciting things happen when this is allowed.

Another possibility is to wonder whether anybody has other stories or associations that could be placed alongside the experience. During the trial of *Living in a fragile world* in the Hereford Diocese, there were some rich and exciting associations made. During the first session, after the world had become a mess and the people seemed to have disappeared under all the destructive forces, somebody remembered the image of the 'remnant' in the Old Testament—the small group of faithful people left after the disaster of the exile. *'There are often more remnants than we think there are. All over the world small groups are trying to make a difference. We must all do something no matter how small. It's just one small step at a time.'*

Another reflection after the trial was that the open 'wondering' process had a more democratic feel than the usual group discussion process. More people contributed than usual and there was a greater feeling of equality of contribution in the group.

It is important to remember, however, that each group will be different, and each time you tell the story it may well be different. You can't predict what will happen. Rejoice and celebrate the learning that takes place when your particular group engages with this material.

Finally… remember to *relax* and *enjoy* this part of the session. *Relax* and *play* with the wondering.

SETTINGS AND VENUES

The *Living in a fragile world* material works best with groups of approximately twelve to fifteen people, although the first session has been presented to just one person with successful results. Equally, the materials may be used with a Key Stage 2 group in a school setting.

You will need an open space to sit in a circle, either on chairs or the floor, with enough space in the circle to spread out the materials. Don't feel cramped. The participants won't want to be too far away; neither will they want to be on top of everything. Groups meeting in houses may well need to be smaller than average.

It's worth taking time, as the storyteller / leader, to arrive well before the session so that the space can be arranged before group members arrive. It doesn't help if chairs are still being arranged as people arrive. The material works best when a sense of drama and expectation is created.

The storyteller will need to operate on the floor.

Some trays or baskets will be useful, so that the materials can be contained.

Sometimes, rather drear and unattractive settings can be made more comfortable by the addition of a rug. Atmospheres can be changed with lighting, candles and nightlights. A vase of flowers, or a few drapes of material hung across old noticeboards, can change the feeling and mood. Use your imagination.

It is helpful to have two people running the session. The second person handles the practicalities, welcoming, notices, refreshments and so on, taking the pressure off the storyteller. This also offers a model of co-operative leadership. The second person may need to give an introduction during the first session, explaining the different style of working, devising the group agreement and so on.

OUTLINE OF THE SESSIONS

The adult group that originally experienced this material met on a weekday during Lent for a period of about one hour and thirty minutes. However, the session very often continued beyond that time. It usually included some follow-up creative activity and a reasonable period of silent prayer.

Some children's groups may have time only for the story and wondering in one week, and will then use the following week to respond with the creative art materials. Some schools exploring the Godly Play model of working have found that giving time to the whole process—the welcome, the story, the wondering, the free creative activity and the sharing of food (usually a whole afternoon)—has had such wonderful benefits that the time has been well spent. In the voluntary sector, a Godly Play session usually takes about an hour.

Different groups will create their own patterns, and different age groups will operate slightly differently. Depending on your resources and situation, you may want to concentrate on the story and wondering time, finishing with a prayer. Be flexible and try different things. The story section may vary, taking anything from ten to twenty-five minutes. Make a note of the time the story takes when you are practising it, and this will help you to plan the overall time of the session.

However, it is important to remember that each of the stories either 'ends in the air' or has an open ending. The questioning time must always follow it, to allow for some resolution, especially when working with children. Within each session you will find suggestions for wondering questions to help you.

those who think that they know everybody. You will also need to remember to do this each week, especially if new people appear. People may need some catch-up time, so a brief résumé of what happened in the previous session might be useful.

Sometimes a short period of silence to recollect the past day, accompanied by some simple relaxation exercises, and followed by a suggestion that people put the busyness of the day aside, can help them to be more present in the group. In the first session, it may be necessary to have a brief introduction to the method and some discussion about group rules (see page 11), so that everybody knows what to expect.

There may be a need for notices and announcements.

You may want to say a short prayer. You may want to include music or a song.

THE STORY

The welcome leads into the presentation of the story. Don't immediately leap in. Leave a silence and get your inner self ready. Don't be pressurized. Begin when you think it's right.

If you haven't read the Introduction chapter, then do so now (see pages 11–14). This will give you some important hints and advice.

WELCOME AND ARRIVAL

Don't underestimate the importance of welcome and arrival. This sets the tone for the rest of the session. If the room isn't ready, and you are still rushing around getting prepared, it will take some time to recover. It's best to have everything ready before people arrive.

Group members need to feel welcomed and acknowledged. Don't assume that everybody knows everybody else. Some form of introduction is necessary even with

WONDERING QUESTIONS

It's useful to have a brief pause after the story section, especially if the person who told the story is also leading the 'wondering'. The pause will help the leader to change gear and get the feel of things.

If a different person is to lead the open questioning, it might be a good idea if they were sitting next to or opposite the storyteller, ideally operating from the floor as well. Again, if you haven't read the advice on page 13, then do so before you lead the session.

If two different people are going to lead the story and question sessions, it is important that they work together at the preparation stage so that each knows what the other is doing. This will help both leaders in their preparation and planning, and will build their confidence— assuring them that they are not on their own. It also models co-operative learning.

CLEARING AWAY

After the wondering in a Godly Play session, the materials are packed away carefully. Everything is put back in its box, basket or tray and the materials returned to their proper place on a set of shelves.

The clearing up for *Living in a fragile world* is especially important, as there is often quite a diversity of materials. You need to show as much care in the packing away as you do while telling the story. Don't bundle everything together in a heap.

Living in a fragile world has been cleared away in a variety of settings. It will depend on what you are doing next and how much room you have to work in. Sometimes the material has been left out for the rest of the session and cleared away at the very end. Whenever you clear away, it needs to be done with care and respect.

Clearing up is also an opportunity to refresh people's memories. Different pieces can be named as they are put away. You can perhaps put the pieces away in reverse order so that you remember each element of the story.

Different members of the group can be given different responsibilities, each person collecting the different items for each of the boxes. In the trial, this was the occasion for the comment about holding the stars of the universe (see page 9). It also resulted in a spontaneous question, 'What might we really do to clean up the world?'

ACTIVITIES

During a Godly Play session, there is usually a response period of free creative activity. People identify what they might like to do, working with a wide range of materials such as paints, clay, papers, pens or pencils, all of which are usually kept on shelves. Other activities include the option of working with the boxes and trays of stories from the shelves. Sitting quietly and thinking is another option.

Most children have no problem with working like this and are free of inhibitions when faced with creative materials. They relish the opportunity of choosing for themselves, especially in a formal educational world which becomes increasingly prescriptive. Teenagers also appreciate the freedom of creativity.

Some adults, on the other hand, feel very threatened when confronted with art materials, and deep fears surface of 'not getting it right'. Therefore, some time needs to be given to explain that judgments will not be made about the artwork and that the session is an opportunity to access non-verbal truths.

Of course, the materials can be used to express things in words and writing, which is familiar territory for some people. For others, however, this will be as threatening as non-verbal activity. It will all depend on your group and your particular setting. Whatever the setting, it is worth trying to do some creative work as it often unlocks issues that haven't surfaced. It is also helpful for those who like some quiet time in which to think things through. Sometimes, imagining that you are a person in the story, writing a letter, a poem, or a story of your own, enables more thoughts and associations.

The main task of the leader in this part of the session is to enable the activity to take place, but not to interfere. The aim is to allow space for people to enter more deeply into the experience of the story. It is not helpful to look over people's shoulders and ask questions, or get in the way. Trust the participants to get on with what they have decided to do. The leader's job is to sit still and watch, responding only if people ask for help.

In some adult groups it may help to get over the creative hurdle if you do a group art exercise. This very often releases some of the fears about handling the materials.

Here is one exercise that might help.

Take a line for a walk

Provide a large piece of paper, big enough for the whole group to work on. You may have to glue several sheets together. Have available a wide range of oil pastels, which have rich and deep colours (crayons are a second best). Each person chooses one or two of the pastels, their favourite colours. They then draw meandering lines across the paper, taking their lines for a walk. Where the lines intersect, irregular spaces are created. Using a wide variety of coloured pastels, each of the sections and spaces can then be filled with graffiti, blocks of colour, patterns, symbols or images that represent different parts of the experience. People can be encouraged to change the colours between different sections. At the end of the exercise, a very light wash of a water-based paint applied with broad brushes adds another dimension: the wax of the pastels resists the water. (Keep the paint thin and watery.)

Someone leads the group, offering different suggestions, such as: *'Fill in a space that represents... your feelings during the last thirty minutes... your hopes... something you would like to say... an image that has stayed in your mind... something that you would like to question... the part you would like to leave out'*, and so on.

Once you get going, different members of the group may well come up with suggestions for ways to fill in the spaces. This exercise can also be done individually on a smaller scale with a sheet of A4 paper. At the end, you may want to spend some time offering people an opportunity to express any new insights, confirmation of thoughts, new questions and so on.

PRAYER AND MEDITATION

For the first group that used this material, prayer and meditation were an important part of the session. They asked for a considerable time of silence to follow the questioning. The visual material was not cleared away and people gathered around it to sit quietly and pray and meditate. They asked for the lights to be switched off, and for nightlights and candles to be lit and placed around the material.

Experience has shown that not only adults but also children and teenagers respond to this opportunity in a deep and profound way. Even very young children can cope with silence when the atmosphere and expectation have been created. This is the time to bring insights and thoughts, issues and needs into the presence of God. It is also the opportunity to receive from God the commission of love for creation and the commission for action to enable that love.

The experience of silence and prayer may bring to the surface yet more insights and possibilities. People may wish to voice concerns and thoughts to God in their own words.

It may be that someone ends this time with a short collect or prayer. A simple phrase such as, *'Lord in your mercy, hear our prayer'* may suffice.

At the end of a period of prayer or meditation, it is not helpful to switch on the lights quickly all at once. Do it gradually, one at a time. If candles have been lit, they can be extinguished carefully. A simple phrase helps to bring people back—for example, *'When you are ready, open your eyes and remember that you are in this room.'*

REFRESHMENTS

You decide when is the most appropriate time for refreshments. Whatever you decide, make sure that someone other than the session leaders is responsible for them. If possible, make something special of the refreshment time: don't tag it on to another part of the session. There's something sacramental about sharing food with one another and focusing on it as an important part of the meeting.

The quality of relationship in which the food is shared is important, not the quantity of food provided. During a visit to Tanzania, in a tiny village dwelling, the sharing of a bottle of soft drink and the passing around of a bowl of nuts took on enormous significance for me. In a place where resources are scarce, the generosity of hospitality and the sense of community were evident and profound.

The sharing of food together while using the *Living in a fragile world* material may also unlock some associations and learning.

ENDING AND DEPARTURE

Give some thought to how the session might end.

- The period of prayer and meditation might form a natural conclusion.
- There might be some announcements for the next week.
- You may want to summarize the important and significant parts of the evening.
- You may want to thank the group for the experience and the learning.

Whatever you do, let people know that the session has ended, so that those who have other commitments can feel free to leave.

MATERIALS AND PATTERNS

Preparation is the key word for this course, and the sessions won't work without it. But preparation can be fun! Don't see it as a chore but as an opportunity. You don't have to do it on your own. In fact, it's preferable if you work and prepare together with another person or a group.

Each session depends on using some specific prepared visual aids to help the stories emerge for the participants. The visual material speaks as loudly as the words. Before you begin to prepare the visual aids, it would be worth reading the scripts several times so that you get an overview of what each one is about.

The actual making of the materials is an important part of the process because it affirms the playful nature of the material. In the making, you are given the opportunity to discover the different and separate elements of the session, and to begin the process of feeling comfortable with the words and structure.

In the making, you will have an opportunity to experiment with what works best for you. It also introduces you to the handling of the material—to experience the feel of it all.

As you play with the raw materials and mould them into shape, it gives you an opportunity to reflect on the overall theme of creation and your responsibility in it.

In the process of making, other thoughts and associations may also arise. You may find that there are better ways of doing it. You may find that you are creating other stories, stimulated by the materials. The whole point is to enjoy it, to play with it and to see the possibilities. In other words, you learn by doing.

The fact that you have given time and skill to the making of the materials seems to make a difference. Beautiful and carefully made materials give the sessions value and capture people's attention.

It is possible for just one person to make the visual aids, but this is not the only option. Other people can be included. Questions to keep asking during the preparation are 'Who else needs to know about this? Who else can be included in this process?'

The making could be:

- a collaborative venture
- an all-age venture
- a community venture

You may need someone to oversee and provide some quality assurance.

The making could be a time of planning and anticipation.

THE VISUAL PARTS OF THE STORIES

The following instructions and patterns are for the visual aids used in the scripts. They are used in each session but in a variety of ways. Some sessions may need additional material, which will be listed at the end of this chapter and the beginning of each script.

The universe cloth

The universe cloth is used at the beginning of each session.

You will need:
- ★ 1.5–2 metres of dark blue or black velvety material, about 110–120cm wide. It's sometimes helpful to have this fabric wrapped around a broom handle.
- ★ A beautiful box, filled with star-shaped sequins. You can buy the sequins from craft shops and sometimes discount bookshops.

The world circle

You will need:
- ★ A good metre of 1.2m-wide strong cotton or calico
- ★ Fabric paints or dyes as described below

If you use calico, it might be best to buy a length of 1.5 metres to allow for shrinkage. Wash the material in hot soapy water before use.

The world circle should be about 1 metre in diameter, but don't cut out your circle at this point. Keep the material as a rectangle while you paint or dye it. The finished product should look like a swirling mass of light blue, rather like the view of the world from space.

To create this effect, use any or all of the following techniques:

- Decorate with different shades of fabric paint. You can buy this in small pots from an art shop. Three pots will be plenty—blue, turquoise and white. Fabric paints are made permanent and washproof by ironing with a hot iron on the wrong side of the material when dry. Instructions should come with the paints.

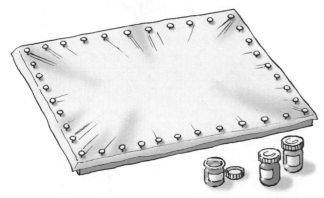

- It's easier to paint material if it is stretched tightly. You could make a simple frame from wood, slightly smaller than the material, and then pin the material on to it with drawing pins or staples. Start with a pin in the middle of one side. Pull the material tightly and add further pins about 2cm apart. Stretch the material tightly and pin the opposite side. Repeat the process with the other edges. The fabric should be as tight as a drum.

  A less satisfactory method is to pin a piece of plastic sheeting to a board or the floor and then stretch the material to the plastic, using masking tape. However, with this method less paint will be absorbed by the material, creating puddles underneath.

- Painting on wet and dry material can make different effects. Mixing the paints also creates a variety of shades. Mixing water with the paints creates lighter shades. You may want to experiment first with smaller pieces of material, but don't throw these away as they may be useful later, for making patchwork.

- Hot and cold water dyes can be brought from chemists and art shops. Follow the instructions on the dye pots. Screw the material up, tie it with string, then immerse it in the dye bath. Untie and repeat, using a different shade of dye. This is less predictable than using fabric paint, but you could always add paint afterwards to touch up and create the desired effect. If you use cold water dye, strong elastic bands can be used instead of string.

- You could also use acrylic paints to create colour washes, with permanent felt pens for extra details. However, this makes the material stiff and less pliable and, when the fabric is folded, may create permanent fold marks.

When you are happy with the effect you have created, make the circle. First, stretch the material tight with pins or tape. Use string, a pencil and a drawing-pin to mark out the circle, as described below. To make a circle 1 metre in diameter, the string (which is the radius) should be about 50cm long, with some extra length to attach to the drawing-pin and pencil.

- Loop one end of the string round the drawing-pin, and stick the pin in the centre of the stretched fabric.
- Loop the other end of the string around the pencil.
- Keeping the string taut and the pencil vertical, draw your circle.
- It may be that some parts of the finished painting or dyeing are better than others. Make sure that the circle includes the appropriate part.
- Unpin the material, cut the circle out carefully and finally zigzag the edges on a sewing machine to prevent fraying.

19

The continent shapes

You will need:

☆ Squares of patterned or plain cotton, mainly in shades of rich green with the occasional autumnal colour. It might be useful to include some icy colours for the two poles.
(Don't worry about deserts as these are created later by laying on separate brown / grey felt hexagons.)

☆ Dark blue felt

The continent shapes are built in patchwork using individual hexagons (each side 3cm). You will find the pattern on page 57. Many fabric shops now sell squares of vibrant-coloured material for patchwork. You could also use scraps of old cotton clothes—even the most faded and dull colours can be enlivened with fabric paints or dyes. It's best to use roughly the same weight of material for all the hexagons.

Alternatively, you could use painted calico or cotton to make the continent shapes. You will need to zigzag the hems on a sewing machine. You may have some scraps of blue calico left over from your paint experiments. These can be repainted or redyed.

The patchwork gives the rough shape of the continents—they don't need to be exact.

You'll also need to make approximately ten single hexagons to represent islands around the world.

The island and continent shapes are backed with dark blue felt. This enables them to be used in different ways with different stories. Sometimes they represent the continents, sometimes the land in general, and sometimes they are turned over to create abstract boundaries and borders.

Follow the patterns opposite for assembling the continent shapes.

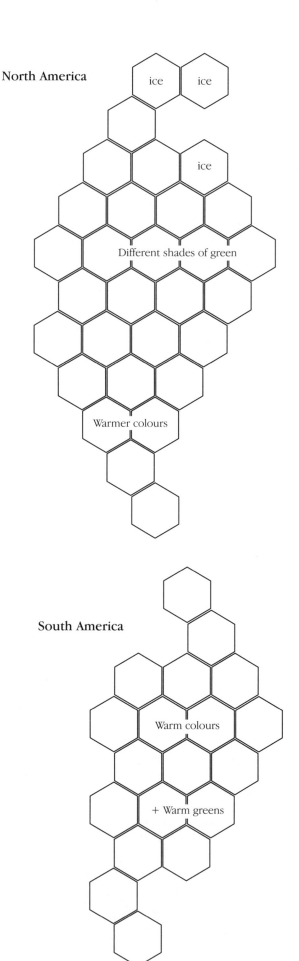

North America

ice   ice

ice

Different shades of green

Warmer colours

South America

Warm colours

+ Warm greens

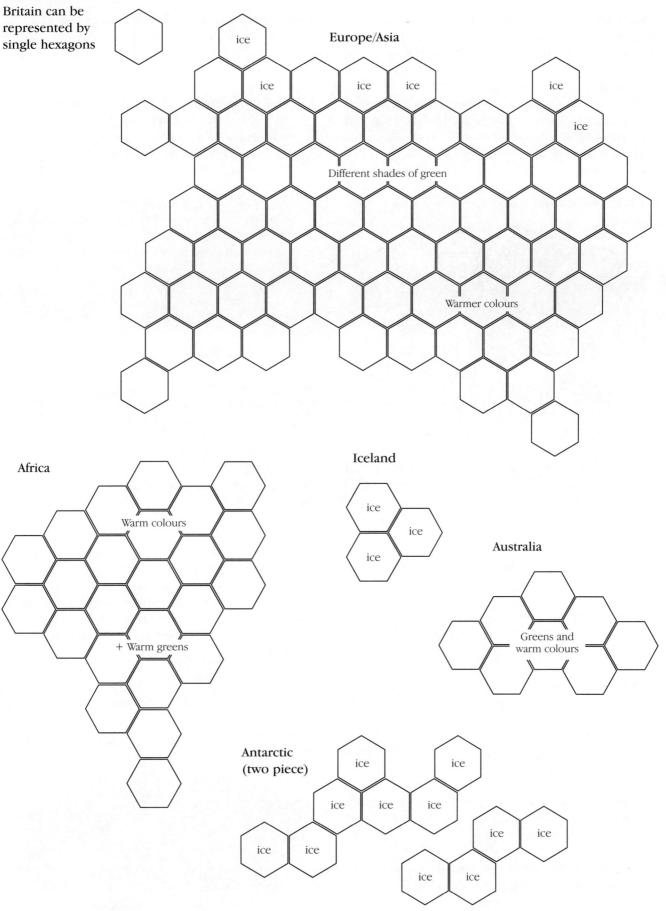

Islands such as Britain can be represented by single hexagons

Europe/Asia

ice

ice ice ice

ice

ice

Different shades of green

Warmer colours

Africa

Warm colours

+ Warm greens

Iceland

ice

ice

ice

Australia

Greens and warm colours

Antarctic (two piece)

ice ice

ice ice ice

ice ice

ice ice

ice ice

21

The things that go bump in the night

The 'things that go bump in the night' are the destructive forces that spoil the world. These are represented in a series of small boxes or bags in sombre colours, each holding a different set of objects. There are ten in total.

Many craft shops stock a selection of different-shaped card boxes, which can then be painted and decorated. If you cannot obtain any, you could make a series of small drawstring bags using darker, sombre colours. Either dye or fabric-paint calico, old clothes or soft furnishings fabrics. Different weights of material can be used. Each bag needs to be about 10cm x 15cm.

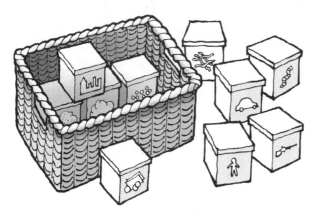

The bags or boxes are kept together in a larger gift box, an open basket or a tray. You may want to put a symbol on each of the separate boxes or bags to remind you of what's inside.

The ten 'things that go bump in the night' are as follows. A variety of these are used in the sessions.

1 **Cities**: You will need approximately twenty small logos representing cities. Use computer clip-art printed on to thin card.

2 **Deserts**: Fill your box or bag with grey or brown felt hexagons, made to the same dimensions as the continent patchwork pieces (each side 3cm long).

3 **People**: Using newspaper or coloured paper, cut out lots of paper-chain people. You will find the pattern on page 59.

4 **Money**: Fill the box or bag with Monopoly paper money or toy money.

5 **Cars**: Fill the box or bag with individual car pictures from magazines mounted on to card. You'll need enough to fill the continents.

6 **CO_2**: Use a large piece of raw sheep's fleece dyed grey or, alternatively, tangled grey wool and strips of frayed grey fabric.

7 **Pesticide**: Fill the box or bag with multi-coloured hole-punch shapes.

8 **Contaminated water**: Fill the box or bag with long strips of wool and thin strips of cotton fabric, using mainly blue, grey and white. Include a few hints of red and yellow.

9 **Viruses and images of disease**: Use long strips of crocheted wool in different colours—for example:
    TB: grey
    AIDS, malaria and measles: red
    Cigarettes and smoke: dark yellow and brown

10 **War**: Some computer clip-art shows pictures of tanks. Print them on to thin card and cut them out. Otherwise, look for images that suggest war. You need to include at least one image of a gun, which will be used in Session Two.

People figures

You will need a basket of people figures for each session. Among them is the universe figure, which is used each time for the first part of the story. This figure has outstretched arms and represents every person. In Session Five it becomes the figure of the Christ. Use the template on page 57 for this figure.

The rest of the people are represented by 15–20 figures of different shapes and sizes. You will find the templates on page 58. Keep the figures simple so that they can mean different things to different people. Cut them from strong art board. Use a craft knife, rather than scissors, to produce cleaner edges, and paint the figures with acrylic paint. Alternatively, make the figures from thin plywood and then use acrylic paint or woodstain to colour them.

Baskets or trays

A selection of open baskets will be useful to keep all the different visual aids tidy and contained.

OTHER MATERIALS NEEDED FOR THE SESSIONS

Session One

You will need:
- ✯ A selection of fish shapes cut out from blue felt or silver card, to scatter in the oceans
- ✯ Some pictures of animals to lay out on the continents

You will find templates for the above items in Appendix One, page 59.

Session Two

You will need:
- ✯ A selection of wooden building bricks of different sizes, including some squares, triangles and rectangles, in order to build some houses, churches and schools. Alternatively, you could cut out shapes to represent the different buildings and mount them on to card.
- ✯ A selection of farm animals, for example, cows, sheep, hens, pigs, plus a workhorse and some tractors, and a selection of hedgerow animals such as birds and rabbits. See Appendix One, pages 60–62, for templates. Alternatively, they can be purchased from a toy or model shop, or you could use pictures mounted on to card.
- ✯ Pictures of food—vegetables and cereals—mounted on to cards. These can be cut from magazines and catalogues. Some florists sell small model versions of apples and vegetables which could be used as an alternative. Templates for food pictures can also be found in Appendix One, page 61.
- ✯ Sheets of A4 paper cut into four to represent the phrase 'ploughed under with paperwork'
- ✯ Some green strips of felt or other material to represent hedges

Session Three

You will need:
- ✯ Different-sized beads threaded on to string or wire about a metre long and tied at both ends.
- ✯ A large pair of scissors to cut the string or wire.

Session Four

No additional items are needed for this session.

Session Five

This session tells the Easter story.

You will need the following household objects. Try to keep the number of objects to the same number as the boxes or bags used in the other four sessions (that is, ten items).

1. A bowl of water and a towel
2. A hammer and some large nails
3. A small glass bowl or vial of scented oil
4. A palm cross or piece of greenery from the garden
5. Thirty silver coins in a small box and a picture of a cockerel
6. A folded white sheet
7. Some vinegar placed in a small glass bottle
8. Some wine in a small corked glass bottle, and a piece of bread, placed together in a basket
9. Some brambles entwined to make a crown
10. An egg, either hard-boiled or, preferably, blown and decorated

Other items that may be used include a large stone, a red or purple robe, or any other object that suggests part of the Easter story.

CREATIVE MATERIALS

If you are going to offer some creative work, it is helpful to have a selection of different paints, crayons, pastels, pens, pencils, glue, scissors, brushes, water pots and different-sized quality papers for painting and writing. Some newspaper is also handy. If you can get some clay, this is a really good medium for exploring the issues. If you have clay available, you will need some boards on which to work and perhaps some sheets of plastic. Some craft shops sell small packets of modelling clay that is less messy than the traditional type, but works just as well.

All the art materials should be arranged carefully and neatly so that participants can access them when they are needed. It is also useful to have someone supervising this area, to provide help if needed.

PART TWO

'LIVING IN A FRAGILE WORLD' STORY SCRIPTS AND WONDERING QUESTIONS

If you haven't read Part One, then do so now.
You will need the information in order to tell the stories.

SESSION ONE

You will need the universe material:

★ The roll of black velvet
★ The box of star sequins
★ The universe figure (the person with outstretched arms)
★ The world circle (rolled into the end of the black velvet so that when the velvet is finally rolled out, planet earth appears at the end)
★ A basket containing the patchwork continent shapes
★ The basket of people figures
★ A basket or gift box containing the 'bump in the night' boxes or bags

You will also need:

★ The basket of blue felt fish shapes to scatter in the oceans
★ Some animal shapes to accompany the people figures

THE STORY

The first part of the story is used first in this session and then repeated in Sessions Two and Four. You will therefore find the script repeated at the head of these sessions. You may like to vary the wording each time to keep it fresh, but it is intended to be a unifying element for each of the sessions. In trials, each age group has enjoyed the repetition of this section, as it helps to create a feeling of familiarity each time. This first part of the story also stands on its own and can be used in a variety of settings, such as assemblies, all-age worship, as an opening for meditation and prayer, story times and many more.

As you lay out part of the roll of black velvet, say…	I wonder if you've ever stood and looked at the night sky and wondered how big it is…. how far it stretches… how immense the universe is…
Scatter sequins during next part— deliberately and gently and with slow, generous hand movements.	Have you wondered at the beauty of the stars in the sky?
	Or how there are thousands upon thousands of suns, stars, planets and moons… thousands of solar systems and galaxies…?
Take the universe figure and place it in the centre of the universe.	And I wonder how you feel when you look up into the vastness of space and think that you are part of it…
Take one sequin and place it carefully at the heart of the figure.	… and that it is also part of you.
Pause.	
Raise hand in blessing over the sequins…	And God saw all the beauty and vastness of the universe and said, 'That's good.'
Unroll more of the black velvet slowly (but keep the last part rolled up, hiding the world circle), saying…	Some people say that the universe may roll on for ever… and there are large parts of it that we will never see or understand.
Pick up one small blue sequin, place it in the palm of your hand, and say…	In the vastness of space, there was one small and minute planet, and it was so beautiful.
Raise other hand in blessing over the sequin and say…	And God said, 'That's good.'
Place the sequin in the middle of the newly laid-out velvet, and unroll the remaining velvet. Unroll the large blue world circle. Place it over the sequin.	

Earth, when seen from space, looks like a great swirling mass of blue, for a large part of it is made up of water…

Bless the planet by raising your hand slowly above the circle of blue.	And God said, 'That's good.'

Reproduced with permission from *Living in a fragile world* published by BRF 2003 (1 84101 325 0)

Lay out patchwork continents and hexagon islands to form a world map. (You could walk your figures across some of the large and small land masses.)

→ As you come closer to earth, you see great masses of wonderfully green fertile land...

Some are so big that it takes months to travel across, but some can be walked across in a few hours...

Scatter the blue felt fish shapes into the oceans.

→ And the oceans teemed with life... with creatures both big and small.

Place animal, bird and people figures on to the continents...

→ And the land was filled with creatures of every kind. And when God saw the world, God laughed and cried and sang for joy, all at the same time, and said...

Bless the world ...

→ 'That's so very good. It's all so very good.'

Sit back and pause.

→ It's time to take a rest.

Place the ten small boxes / bags around the outside of the world, saying...

→ But we live in a fragile world, and sometimes things go bump in the night.

I wonder what these might be. They could be gifts or presents. I wonder if they are.

There are quite a lot of them. I wonder what might be inside...

Open city box and lay out about five small cities.

→ It looks like a set of buildings, like a city.

Some people enjoyed the gift of the city...

Point to two different figures. Place one near a city, the other in the country.

→ ... while others enjoyed the life outside.

Open money box and scatter some money near the cities.	The gift of paper money made life much easier—as paying with gold, or bartering with shells and goods is so complicated.
Open people box and bring out several strings of people.	Look! The number of people is growing… so that new cities have to be built.
Lay more cities down… scatter some more money.	See, the forests are disappearing…
Lay down some grey hexagons—especially in South America.	… and so the animals have no place to live.
Remove some animals.	We'll have to cut down some more forests to make room, but this also makes the deserts bigger.
Using grey hexagons, create the Sahara desert and other desert areas.	
Keep adding people, cities and money—distributing cities and money mainly in the northern hemisphere, but don't forget Australasia!	And still the numbers of people keep growing, so that by now there are over six billion of us… and half of us now live in cities.
Open car box, and scatter cars.	Transport is a wonderful gift. It helps us move from place to place.
	Although some of us have more than one car… some have two… some have more… and some people have none…
Sit back for a moment to survey the whole scene. Then open the CO_2 box, take out the grey smoke and spread it across the continents.	The fumes from the cars and the cities, and the burning of forests, send smoke into the air…
	… that forms a blanket in the air…
Use hand to show heat…	… that heats up the planet… that melts some of the land…
Remove part of Antarctica… use hand to show flood…	… that floods large parts of the earth…
Scatter more money in north.	… that costs millions of pounds to pay for the damage…

 Reproduced with permission from *Living in a fragile world* published by BRF 2003 (1 84101 325 0)

Scoop up a handful of the fish from the sea, and put them into a basket behind you.	Fish are needed to feed the people... The oceans are nearly barren...
Open pesticide box, and scatter liberally across the land.	The land is needed to produce more food, so fertilizer, pesticide and chemicals are scattered to increase the growth...
	... but the rain...
Use hand to denote rain.	... washes them underground and pollutes the waters that have been under the earth for over a thousand years...
Open the water box and pull out the strips of blue cotton. Lay them throughout the oceans and on the continents.	
Open virus box, and lay the viruses alongside the people.	Millions are killed each year from simple diseases, TB, malaria, measles, polluted water, AIDS...
Pause.	... and millions are killed by cigarettes... While many people here...
Point to America and Europe.	... are giving up smoking, the cigarette companies are deliberately trying the hard sell here...
Move cigarette virus to Africa and Asia.	
Pause.	There is one more bag / box...
Open war box, and silently place the tanks and images of war around the world in areas of present-day conflict... Africa, South America, Eastern Europe, Middle East, and so on...	People are struggling to survive...
Pause.	And God looked at the world... and said...
Raise your hand as if to bless—but then hesitate and say...	'That's...'
Pause... then sit back and look up.	

WONDERING QUESTIONS

You don't have use all the wondering questions suggested for this session. Gauge the mood of your group; some of the questions might be appropriate for future sessions. You may also think of your own. It's usually a good idea to end the questioning session when the group energy is high, with a feeling that more could be explored.

★ I wonder which part of the story you liked best…

★ I wonder if there's anything you would like to leave out…

★ I wonder where the changes were in the story…

★ I wonder how you felt at the different parts of this story…

★ I wonder what you feel and think about the boxes / bags…

★ I wonder if there are any more boxes / bags and what they might be…

★ I wonder what might happen next…

★ I wonder how much more the world can take…

★ I wonder if there's a limit…

★ I wonder if it's really like this…

★ I wonder what might be done to change this story…

★ I wonder what we might really do…

★ I wonder what God might to say to the world…

★ I wonder how God feels…

★ I wonder what the world might to say to God…

★ I wonder how the world feels…

Closing this part of the session

When you feel that the energy has gone out of the discussion, you will need to find some way of showing that this part of the session is ending and the next is about to begin. One way is to bring people's attention to the materials.

A simple gesture of the hand can do this, with some simple closing remark or some affirmation about the quality of response. It may be that you suggest a moment of silence to reflect on what has been said. Then move on to give instructions for the next part of your process.

If you decide to put the materials away at this point, turn to page 16 for some suggestions as to how this might be done.

Either at this point or at the very end, when all the materials have been gathered together and replaced into their containers and baskets, you could lay your hands on the materials and say…

God looked at the world and loved it so much…

Reproduced with permission from *Living in a fragile world* published by BRF 2003 (1 84101 325 0)

SESSION TWO

You will need the universe material:

★ The roll of black velvet
★ The box of star sequins
★ The universe figure (the person with outstretched arms)
★ The world circle (rolled into the end of the black velvet so that when the velvet is finally rolled out, planet earth appears at the end)
★ A basket containing the patchwork continent shapes
★ The basket of people figures
★ A basket or gift box containing the 'bump in the night' boxes or bags

You will also need:

★ The baskets with the wooden bricks or buildings pictures
★ The figures or pictures of animals and birds
★ The pictures of food and crops
★ The sheets of A4 paper cut into four to represent the phrase, 'ploughed under with paperwork'
★ The green strips of felt that represent hedges

THE STORY

This story explores the story of the countryside. It came out of the experience of a rural part of England at the beginning of the millennium. Much of the wording comes from the insights given by children and adults from the area, gathered in a project that listened to their stories of daily living. The foot and mouth crisis was the culmination of that experience. People from urban and non-rural settings are encouraged to use this story. It may well be that we share common themes and stories. There will also be differences. Having told this story, you may want to devise your own for your own setting with your symbols and objects. I hope that you will do so.

Repeat the first part of the story from Session One as set out opposite. Continue until the blue circle of the world is rolled out. It may be appropriate to alter the wording slightly in order to create a freshness.

As you lay out part of the roll of black velvet, say…	I wonder if you've ever stood and looked at the night sky and wondered how big it is… how far it stretches… how immense the universe is…
Scatter sequins during next part—deliberately and gently and with slow, generous hand movements.	Have you wondered at the beauty of the stars in the sky? Or how there are thousands upon thousands of suns, stars, planets and moons… thousands of solar systems and galaxies…
Take the universe figure and place it in the centre of the universe.	And I wonder how you feel when you look up into the vastness of space and think that you are part of it…
Take one sequin and place it carefully at the heart of the figure.	… and that it is also part of you.
Pause.	
Raise hand in blessing over the sequins…	And God saw all the beauty and vastness of the universe and said, 'That's good.'
Unroll more of the black velvet slowly (but keep the last part rolled up, hiding the world circle), saying…	Some people say that the universe may roll on for ever… and there are large parts of it that we will never see or understand.
Pick up one small blue sequin, place it in the palm of your hand, and say…	In the vastness of space, there was one small and minute planet, and it was so beautiful.
Raise other hand in blessing over the sequin and say…	And God said, 'That's good.'
Place the sequin in the middle of the newly laid-out velvet, and unroll the remaining velvet. Unroll the large blue world circle. Place it over the sequin.	

— ⌘ —

Reach over the blue circle.	Last week we imagined that we looked at the world from a distance… as if we were hovering in the skies. We saw what was happening to the world… This week we are going to come down to earth and put our feet on to the ground…

Reproduced with permission from *Living in a fragile world* published by BRF 2003 (1 84101 325 0)

Take the patchwork continent pieces, and lay them together side by side to make one land mass. Some of the individual hexagons can be used to fill gaps and make a more interesting shape. As you arrange them, say…	This is not the land that is far away in other countries… or far away to the east or west or north or south… It is the land from around here *(or from our country)* … the land of our place… covered with a patchwork of fields…
Place the wooden bricks into groups.	Here are the settlements and villages…
Name the buildings.	… houses… school… church…
Place some isolated bricks nearby.	… barns… farms…
Add hedge pieces.	… and hedges…
Add farm animals, wild animals and birds.	The land sustained a rich mix of creatures…
Add a few of the people figures.	… and people…
Point to each of the people figures.	These are the people of the land… the people of the soil who worked hard together, caring for the crops and animals… providing food for others. The land itself and the stories of their life together enfolded them.
Pass hand around entire scene.	They were bound together and all together.
Join hands together over the scene.	God looked at the people and the creatures, the fields, the villages and the hedgerows and said… 'That's good.' Life on the land was very hard work… harder for some than others… and many were needed for the jobs that had to be done. But when the harvest was finished, the people joined together to sing and dance and thank God for the gifts of creation…
Arrange people in circle by the church.	Work was made easier with some good inventions…
Remove workhorse and replace with a tractor…	

Pause. Then lay down the 'bump in the night' boxes or bags around the edge of the cloth.	But we live in a fragile world, and sometimes things go bump in the night.
Open the cities box and add some city cards to the edges of the countryside.	Cities grew…
Open the money box and place some money by the cities.	… and some people became very rich indeed, so that they began to take over everything…
	They were the people of far away…

You could change your position here—perhaps look up or lean back—but try not to make eye contact with the group (see page 12).	… who soon began to make decisions about how the people of the land should live their lives… decisions often based on how expensive… and how efficient things were…
Spread more money around the edge of the land.	Trains and buses were too expensive to run in the countryside, and so they disappeared.
Move hand across the scene as if taking them away.	So people had to go everywhere by car…
Open car box and place car on patchwork.	And soon cars were the only way to travel…
Scatter more cars over the patchwork.	Some people even had two cars, and some had none…
	Everything began to change. So some of the people of the soil left for the cities to seek their fortune…

 Reproduced with permission from *Living in a fragile world* published by BRF 2003 (1 84101 325 0)

Remove one or two of the figures and place them by the cities.	The villages became smaller, so that some of the buildings fell down or were closed…
Push over barn shape… push down school.	And the children of the village had to travel to school somewhere else…
Take a child figure into the palm of your hand and move it away.	Their life together was not so bound…
Hold hands together and partly pull apart.	
Place some of the figures in the cities.	The lives of the city people were busy and full, but they loved the land as it reminded them of a quieter, more peaceful time…
	Some of them came to live there with the money they had made…
Bring two city figures into the land.	… and they restored the barns…
Replace barn shape.	… and made them into beautiful houses…
Place triangular wood block on top.	Others wanted to live a gentler life, so new buildings were built…
Add new blocks and figures.	
Pause, then point to one of the land people.	We cannot afford to buy houses like this…
Remove figure to city.	… we will go to the city to find our fortune.

Reproduced with permission from *Living in a fragile world* published by BRF 2003 (1 84101 325 0)

Add some more cities.	The people in the cities grew and grew and needed more and more food... so the people from far away... gave orders that there should be bigger and better food... food all the same shape and size...

And the people of the land worked hard to produce it... They took away their hedges so that the tractors could move around more easily... |
Remove two of the three hedges and some wildlife and place them in one of the baskets behind you.	
Bring some of the food pictures to the land, then place them on the edge among the money and city cards.	They spread more pesticide and fertilizer to make the crops grow...
Open fertilizer box and sprinkle over some of the wildlife... then remove more birds and wildlife.	And the land produced more fruit...
Repeat action with food.	Some of the animals were using too much land... it wasn't efficient or economically viable...

So large sheds were built and the animals crowded in. |
Bring two wooden blocks and place chickens and pigs inside and place a lid on top.	
Move hands over countryside and city.	Life everywhere was so busy... everywhere people were so busy working...
Point to some city people.	'We love the peace and tranquillity of the hills and countryside,' said the people of the cities... and more came for visits... to rest and refresh themselves...
Move some figures into the centre and then back again.	The people far away insisted that forms, and more forms, and more forms should be kept. 'We want to know how and when and why and where our food is made... so you must keep a written record.'
Scatter paper over the land... take one of the tractors and move it over the paperwork...	The people of the land said, 'We are ploughed under with paperwork. We cannot do this any more.'

Reproduced with permission from *Living in a fragile world* published by BRF 2003 (1 84101 325 0)

Remove a figure.	The people from far away said, 'We will have a competition to see who can make our food the cheapest.' Soon the cheaper food arrived from other countries.
Add more food. Move it from the outside of the circle.	'We cannot compete,' said the people of the land… So they left the land and sold their houses to those who could afford to buy them… Their young said, 'There are no jobs here for us any more,' and they left for the cities… and their smallholdings were sold and taken into the bigger farms.
Remove people… move smaller patchwork pieces into the large pieces.	The people of the land sometimes felt like strangers in their own communities… One day, the people saw that their cows were sick…
Open virus box and wrap around one of the cows, then lay it on its side.	… and some people said, 'It is the farmers' fault… we shall not buy our meat from here… we'll go to other countries… it's cheaper there.'
Point to figure with arms in air.	'We cannot carry on…'
Open the box with the gun and place on or by the figure… remove figure slowly, gently placing it in the open palm of one hand and raising the other in blessing over it… Gently place it behind you. Bring out another virus… pull over sheep and cattle… gather them up and lay them in a pile… open smoke box and place smoke over the pile… Pause, then sit back.	Then, not long after…

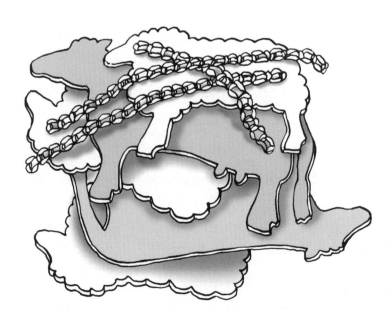

Reproduced with permission from *Living in a fragile world* published by BRF 2003 (1 84101 325 0)

WONDERING QUESTIONS

You don't have use all the wondering questions suggested for this session. Gauge the mood of your group; some of the questions might be appropriate for future sessions. You may also think of your own. It's usually a good idea to end the questioning session when the group energy is high, with a feeling that more could be explored.

⭐ I wonder which part of the story you liked best…

⭐ I wonder if there's anything that we could leave out…

⭐ I wonder why some of the boxes / bags are still closed…

⭐ I wonder what happen if they were opened…

⭐ I wonder how the people of the land feel, living in the city…

⭐ I wonder how the people of the city feel, living on the land…

⭐ I wonder how long it takes to become a person of the land… a person of the city…

⭐ I wonder where home is for both people…

⭐ I wonder if it's really like this…

⭐ I wonder what might happen next…

Closing this part of the session

When you feel that the energy has gone out of the discussion, you will need to find some way of showing that this part of the session is ending and the next is about to begin. One way is to bring people's attention to the materials.

A simple gesture of the hand can do this, with some simple closing remark or some affirmation about the quality of response. It may be that you suggest a moment of silence to reflect on what has been said. Then move on to give instructions for the next part of your process.

If you decide to put the materials away at this point, turn to page 16 for some suggestions as to how this might be done.

Either at this point or at the very end, when all the materials have been gathered together and replaced into their containers and baskets, you could lay your hands on the materials and say…

God looked at the world and loved it so much…

Reproduced with permission from *Living in a fragile world* published by BRF 2003 (1 84101 325 0)

SESSION THREE

You will need the universe material:

⭐ The roll of black velvet

⭐ The box of star sequins

⭐ The universe figure (the person with outstretched arms)

⭐ The world circle (rolled into the end of the black velvet so that when the velvet is finally rolled out, planet earth appears at the end)

⭐ A basket containing the patchwork continent shapes

⭐ The basket of people figures

⭐ A basket or gift box containing the 'bump in the night' boxes or bags

You will also need:

⭐ A collection of different-sized beads threaded on to string or wire about a metre in length and tied at both ends

⭐ A large pair of scissors to cut the string or wire

THE STORY

The material for this section explores the connections and disconnections of our life together in community. Much of the content was inspired by the actual words of adults and children during conversations about what life was like 'living around here'. Participants may well talk about personal experiences during this session. Very often, they don't want answers but safe, secure places in which to offer their experience. The advice for leaders on pages 11–14 offers some guidance as to how safe places are created. It you haven't yet read these pages, please do so now. If you have read them, you may like to refresh your memory.

As a variation on previous weeks, select about ten different sequins and place them in the palm of your hand.

Unroll the universe cloth. → I wonder if you have ever looked at the night sky and seen how big and vast it is... and remembered that at the heart of our solar system is a star that we call the sun...

Place one sequin down... then place the other sequins down one at a time. Space them over the cloth. → ... and that there are thousands of suns in this vast universe...

Our sun has a great family of planets that surround it...

Open the pot of sequins and scatter sequins around one of the suns. → ... circling and spinning in connection with each other... and each of the thousands upon thousands of suns is the same...

Repeat with more sequins around each sun.

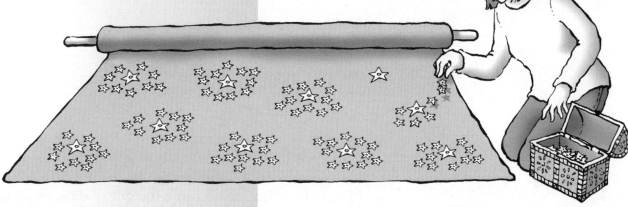

Take the universe figure from its basket, and place it in the universe. → I wonder if you've ever thought that you are part of this great family of the universe...

Take one sequin and place it on the figure. → ... and that the universe is also part of you...

Hold hands in blessing over the material, and say... → And God looked at the connection of all things both great and small and said, 'That's good.'

Unroll more of the universe cloth. Pick up one blue sequin and place it in the centre of the velvet... then unroll the remaining velvet and blue earth circle. → And one small planet in this vast universe was so blue that it swirled with the waters of life, both great... and small...

41

Take the continent pieces and lay them, blue side up, around the edge of the blue world circle, creating an enclosed space of waters. The long strips of the Antarctica pieces are laid down so that they go into the universe. The whole shape should resemble a womb-like shape with an umbilical cord going into the universe.

God moved over the waters and gave them his blessing…

Move hands over the waters and hold them over the material in blessing.

Throughout millions upon millions of years, all manner of living things came from the waters of life, both great and small…

Move hand to indicate life coming up from the water.

… including the gift of humanity…

Take one of the people figures and place it in the palm of your hand and show it to everybody. Place it on the large blue circle of material, towards the edge…

From the waters of life came the young and the old, and the variety of the people in between…

Add other figures around the edges as you say the next part.

Male and female…

… with the rich mix of skin, hair and eye colour, culture and custom…

… the rich mix of shape, size and ability…

From the water of life came the gift of difference, for each is unique…

… and the waters of life bind them together in their common humanity…

The cells of their body and their DNA… binds each to each…

In the centre of the world, lay out seven individual patchwork hexagons—one in the centre, six surrounding it—to represent a human cell.

Circle the scene with your hands.	The circle of life bound them together…
Place the circle of beads around the cell shape. If it is too large, make a double circle.	
As you say the next part, move the figures to form a circle around the beads.	Their common questing and searching for meaning for their place in the universe…
	… their living and dying, their dying and living…
	… called them into the circle of life…
Move hands around the circle.	… as children of God…
	… as children of the universe.
	Together and all together they are bound to God and each other…
Join hands over the circle.	
Pause, then place boxes or bags around the edge.	But we live in a fragile world, and sometimes things go bump in the night…
	Instead of difference being seen as a blessing, some see it as a curse…
Point to one figure.	You are not like me… you are not like us… Leave the circle…
Take a figure and move it aggressively to the edge.	The circle of life is broken…
Take a large pair of scissors, cut the thread and allow the beads to spill everywhere.	

 Reproduced with permission from *Living in a fragile world* published by BRF 2003 (1 84101 325 0)

Repeat pointing and moving action.	→ Your colour, your culture, your gender is in question. You must leave the circle…
Take one of the small figures and hold it gently.	→ Nobody listens to what we have to say… and if they do, they usually laugh…
Move the figure to the edge.	→ … and the laughter pushed them out of the circle…
Open money box.	→ The gift of money was given to help life flow around the circle… but some grabbed more than others…
Distribute money unevenly, also disrupting the circle as you go.	
Open virus box and wrap a virus around one figure.	→ Sometimes sickness brought the memories of the circle back…
Move two figures next to sick person.	→ But sometimes sickness broke the circle even more…
Wrap red virus around another person.	→ … and those who were ill were pushed even further from the circle…
Move figure to edge.	→ People had memories of the circle of life, so they made smaller ones…
Open grey hexagon box and create separate circles around groups.	→ … but they forgot the gift of difference and their circles began to divide the people from each other…
Add more grey hexagons between people.	→ … even to the point where they would destroy one another…
Open the war box and distribute tanks between people.	→ The world was spinning all the time…
Spin hands over the world.	→ … but the people span even faster in their busy lives…
Move figures around the cloth.	→ … for each had forgotten the other…
Pick up a handful of beads and cut thread.	→ … and the things that bound them together into the circle of life.
Lift up one of the figures into a standing position.	→ We are more fragmented than we used to be!

Reproduced with permission from *Living in a fragile world* published by BRF 2003 (1 84101 325 0)

WONDERING QUESTIONS

You don't have use all the wondering questions suggested for this session. Gauge the mood of your group; some of the questions might be appropriate for future sessions. You may also think of your own. It's usually a good idea to end the questioning session when the group energy is high, with a feeling that more could be explored.

☆ I wonder which part of this story you liked best...

☆ I wonder which part you would leave out...

☆ I wonder what it might be like to be born in the water of life...

☆ I wonder how it feels to be part of the vast universe...

☆ I wonder how it feels to be pushed out of the circle...

☆ I wonder why some people find it hard to live with difference...

☆ I wonder if it's really like this...

☆ I wonder how the circle of life might be repaired...

☆ I wonder where you fit into this story...

☆ I wonder if anything else goes 'bump in the night'...

☆ I wonder what conflicts go on around here...

☆ I wonder how this story ends...

Closing this part of the session

When you feel that the energy has gone out of the discussion, you will need to find some way of showing that this part of the session is ending and the next is about to begin. One way is to bring people's attention to the materials.

A simple gesture of the hand can do this, with some simple closing remark or some affirmation about the quality of response. It may be that you suggest a moment of silence to reflect on what has been said. Then move on to give instructions for the next part of your process.

If you decide to put the materials away at this point, turn to page 16 for some suggestions as to how this might be done.

Either at this point or at the very end, when all the materials have been gathered together and replaced into their containers and baskets, you could lay your hands on the materials and say...

God looked at the world and loved it so much...

 Reproduced with permission from *Living in a fragile world* published by BRF 2003 (1 84101 325 0)

SESSION FOUR

You will need the universe material:
- ☆ The roll of black velvet
- ☆ The box of star sequins
- ☆ The universe figure (the person with outstretched arms)
- ☆ The world circle (rolled into the end of the black velvet so that when the velvet is finally rolled out, planet earth appears at the end)
- ☆ A basket containing the patchwork continent shapes
- ☆ The basket of people figures
- ☆ A basket or gift box containing the 'bump in the night' boxes or bags

Have the basket of people available. You won't need it for the story but it might be needed for the questioning part of the session.

Repeat the first part of the universe story as in previous weeks. As before, the style of telling is slow, meditative and deliberate.

THE STORY

This story revisits some of the previous material and offers an opportunity for people to link this with their own experience. The four stories offer different perspectives—the cosmic and world viewpoints set alongside local and community experiences. The purpose of this section is summed up in the words 'I wonder whether you have thought that you are part of the world and the world is part of you'.

As you lay out part of the roll of black velvet, say…	I wonder if you've ever stood and looked at the night sky and wondered how big it is… how far it stretches… how immense the universe is…
Scatter sequins during next part—deliberately and gently and with slow, generous hand movements.	Have you wondered at the beauty of the stars in the sky? Or how there are thousands upon thousands of suns, stars, planets and moons… thousands of solar systems and galaxies…
Take the universe figure and place it in the centre of the universe.	And I wonder how you feel when you look up into the vastness of space and think that you are part of it…
Take one sequin and place it carefully at the heart of the figure.	… and that it is also part of you.
Pause.	
Raise hand in blessing over the sequins…	And God saw all the beauty and vastness of the universe and said, 'That's good.'
Unroll more of the black velvet slowly (but keep the last part rolled up, hiding the world circle), saying…	Some people say that the universe may roll on for ever… and there are large parts of it that we will never see or understand.
Pick up one small blue sequin, place it in the palm of your hand, and say…	In the vastness of space, there was one small and minute planet, and it was so beautiful.
Raise other hand in blessing over the sequin and say…	And God said, 'That's good.'
Place the sequin in the middle of the newly laid-out velvet, and unroll the remaining velvet. Unroll the large blue world circle. Place it over the sequin.	

 Reproduced with permission from *Living in a fragile world* published by BRF 2003 (1 84101 325 0)

When you have rolled out the blue planet circle, lay out the continent pieces blue side up, as last week. Take the person figure from the universe and lay it in the centre of the blue circle, with the sequin at the heart. You may need to rearrange the continent pieces slightly.

I wonder whether you have thought that you are part of the world, and the world is part of you.

Take about seven or eight of the sequins from the universe, or from the box, and create a circle around the figure. The sequins will be removed one at a time as you continue the story, but there should be at least one left at the end, so work this out in your practice run.

Sometimes the light of the universe stays with you and surrounds you with life.

Sit back and pause... then place the 'bump in the night' bags or boxes in a circle around the edge.

But we live in a fragile world, and sometimes things go bump in the night.

Open the sickness box and lay out some of the contents.

Illness and sickness may come to us. It could be a cold or a headache. It could be something far more serious...

Remove one of the sequins from around the figure and replace it into the box.

And it feels as if some of the life and the light goes...

Open the fertilizer box and scatter some contents to the side.

Fertilizer is used to make the crops grow well... but some makes the plants and the animals sick and some of them die.

Reproduced with permission from *Living in a fragile world* published by BRF 2003 (1 84101 325 0)

Remove a sequin as before.	And it feels as if some of the life and the light goes…
Open the water box and lay the contents beside it.	Many in the world have no clean water to drink and become so ill that some of us die.
Remove another sequin.	And it feels as if the light and the life goes…
Open the money box / bag and lay out the contents.	Money, money and more money. The more you get, the more you want…
	… and sometimes it rules our lives.
Remove another sequin.	And it feels as if the light and the life goes…
Open the car box and lay some of the contents to the side.	Cars—they can be so useful, but for some they are weapons of destruction and fear…
Open the fumes box.	… and their fumes can make breathing and life so hard.
Remove another sequin.	And it feels as if the light and the life goes…
Open the cities box and lay out some contents.	Cities are filled with people and energy.
	They are also places of loneliness and isolation.
Open the desert box and lay some of the pieces by the city.	Sometimes they feel like places of wilderness and desert.
Remove a sequin.	And it feels as if the light and the life goes…
Open the war box and lay some of the contents to the side.	Conflicts great and small, at home or abroad…
Open the people box and separate out some of the figures.	… tear people apart, tear the world apart.
	War within tears us apart.
Remove the sequin from the heart of the person.	And it feels as if the light and the life goes…
Sit back and pause.	

WONDERING QUESTIONS

You don't have use all the wondering questions suggested for this session. Gauge the mood of your group; some of them might be appropriate for future sessions. You may also think of your own. It's usually a good idea to end the questioning session when the group energy is high, with a feeling that more could be explored.

★ I wonder which part of this story you liked best...

★ I wonder which part you would like to leave out...

★ I wonder which part you thought was the most important...

★ I wonder how it felt when the light and life were taken away...

★ I wonder if you are in this story...

★ I wonder if this story can be done differently or arranged differently... (You may need the other figures for this part.)

★ I wonder if there are any important parts of this story that are missing...

★ I wonder how the light and life might be returned...

★ I wonder how much light and life there really is...

★ I wonder how the story really ends...

★ I wonder if you know of any other stories that could be put alongside this one...

★ I wonder if this is a real story...

Closing this part of the session

When you feel that the energy has gone out of the discussion, you will need to find some way of showing that this part of the session is ending and the next is about to begin. One way is to bring people's attention to the materials.

A simple gesture of the hand can do this, with some simple closing remark or some affirmation about the quality of response. It may be that you suggest a moment of silence to reflect on what has been said. Then move on to give instructions for the next part of your process.

If you decide to put the materials away at this point, turn to page 16 for some suggestions as to how this might be done.

Either at this point or at the very end, when all the materials have been gathered together and replaced into their containers and baskets, you could lay your hands on the materials and say...

God looked at the world and loved it so much...

SESSION FIVE

This session tells the Easter story using the same material.

You will need the universe material:
- ✮ The roll of black velvet
- ✮ The box of star sequins
- ✮ The universe figure
- ✮ The world circle (roll the blue world circle into the end of the black velvet so that when the velvet is finally rolled out, planet earth appears at the end)
- ✮ A basket containing the patchwork continent shapes, colourful side up

Have the basket of figures and the 'bump in the night' material available. You won't need these for the story but they need to be visible during the questioning session.

You will also need:
- ✮ A basket with the household objects to tell the Easter story (see page 23)

THE STORY

This final story makes links between the previous material and the story of Christ. The aim of this session is to create space for people to make connections. The role of the leader is to enable rather than dictate, so resist the temptation to fill in the gaps. Let the group make connections that are right for them.

The material offers two options after the introduction, one that is free and one that is directed. You could create a third, which might incorporate elements of both.

The second option could be used in a variety of settings and times. It has been used with parents and children at an end-of-term service at Easter.

Unroll the velvet as before and place the universe figure towards the side, in a place where it won't be covered up when the blue circle is laid out.	**There was once someone who loved to look at the night sky and see how beautiful and vast it was…**
Slowly spread sequins as before. Leave a space for some silence.	**And as he looked, he knew that he wasn't alone, for he knew that in the vastness and greatness of everything, God was very close.**
	And as he looked, he knew that he was part of the universe…
Place a sequin on the heart.	**… and that the universe was part of him.**
Lay out the blue circle and place the continent shapes, colourful side up, around the edges of the circle, leaving a large space in the centre of the circle.	
Gently take the figure into the palm of your hand. Try to keep the sequin in place, and show it to each member of the group as you say…	**And he not only loved the beauty of the universe, but he loved the world so much as well. He loved it so much that he knew that he was part of the world and that the world was part of him.**
Lay the figure in the centre of the world circle.	**Because he loved the world so much, he also knew how fragile it all is, and about the things that go bump in the night.**
Take the basket with the Easter objects and place them around the edge of the world circle.	

There are now two options you could take.

Option One

Place the objects randomly, and spend some time wondering with the group what they might be—what this story might be about. It doesn't matter whether people get the story in the right order. At this stage explore the different elements. The beauty of this method is that very often the different objects will have more than one association; for example, the water not only becomes Jesus washing the feet of the disciples, but also Pilate washing his hands.

When all have made a contribution, the task is then to fill in some missing details and spend some time wondering in which order, and how, the objects might be arranged.

Don't underestimate people's knowledge—they often know more than you think. Remember the rules of affirming what people say. A useful phrase is, 'Yes, it could be that… It could be lots of things… Here is another thing it could be.' This freer method often brings a wealth of possibilities that you might not have thought of.

Reproduced with permission from *Living in a fragile world* published by BRF 2003 (1 84101 325 0)

Option Two: A more directive approach

Lay the objects around the edge in order: the palm cross, or greenery... the towel and water... the bread and wine... the silver coins and cockerel... a crown of thorns... the hammer and nails... the vinegar... the scented oil... the white sheet... the egg. The egg completes the circle and links up with the palm cross or greenery.

For each section of the story, either point to the object or hold it in your hand and bring it close to the central figure, then replace it. Remember to do this with grace and gentleness.

Indicate the palm cross. → Here are the branches of greenery that people waved as they cheered 'Hosanna' at the beginning of the week. But he knew that the cheers would soon turn to shouts of hate. He knew that in this fragile world things would go bump in the night.

Indicate the water and towel. → Some of the story says that on the night before he died, he called his friends together and washed their feet. He dried them with a towel, and said, 'You are to love one another as I love you.'

Indicate the bread and wine. → Another part of the story says that he then took some bread, blessed it, broke it, and gave them some to eat. He did the same with the wine. 'Remember me when you eat and drink this... because I'll always be with you.'

Indicate the money and cockerel. → Then more things went bump in the night. They left the room of the supper and went to the garden of Gethsemane... There the soldiers arrested him. His friends ran away... One of them, so they say, took money to betray him... Another said, 'He's not my friend'... and a cockerel crew... and the friend wept bitterly.

Indicate the crown of thorns.	The rulers were afraid of him. They wanted him gone, and said he must die. He had talked about a kingdom... the kingdom of heaven... a kingdom of love... a kingdom of peace... But many people didn't understand what he said, so they made a crown of thorns and laughed in his face.
Indicate the hammer and nails.	He was taken away and nailed to a cross... Some stories say that he now knew the real things that go bump in the night.
Indicate the vinegar.	In one of the stories, it says that a soldier nearby heard him groan. So the soldier took a sponge, soaked it in vinegar and herbs, and gave him a drink. Soon afterwards he gave up his spirit and died.
Remove the sequin.	
Indicate the scented oil.	Some friends nearby, mainly women, took his body down from the cross, and some stories say that they anointed it with sweet-smelling spices...
Take the figure in your hand. As you pick up the folded sheet, hide the figure in one of the folds and replace the sheet in its place in the circle.	... then they wrapped it in a sheet and took it to a cave where a large stone was placed over the front. And they thought that he was gone for ever... ... from the world... from the universe.
Motion your hand over the whole scene and pause...	
Then bring the egg to the centre.	But things that are dead also bring life. Some stories say that three days later the stone from the cave was moved away and that the one who was dead was also alive.
Bring the figure back to the centre from the folds of the sheet.	Not only alive but, in some way, always alive, for ever more... and that the life and light will always be there.
Return sequin to figure.	

Take the figure in your palm and show it to everybody as you say the following.

Move hand around the circle of objects several times.

There was once someone who knew that they were part of the universe and that the universe was part of them…

… who knew that they were part of the world and that the world was part of them…

There was once someone who loved the universe so much…

… who loved the world so much…

… that they knew how fragile it all was, and about the things that go bump in the night…

And so the story goes on… around and around.

The following section could either be used after the story and before the questioning or be used after the period of questioning to lead into a time of quiet prayer and meditation. It links the images that have been used throughout the stories. Sometimes a very quiet piece of music can be played to cover people's movement.

Pause.

Pick up the box of sequins and place them in front of the group. Then say something like…

Many people think that this is a very precious story, a story of great value. I wonder if you would like to put some sequins on the parts of the story you think are most precious to you…

Pause.

Reproduced with permission from *Living in a fragile world* published by BRF 2003 (1 84101 325 0)

WONDERING QUESTIONS

You don't have use all the wondering questions suggested for this session. Gauge the mood of your group; some of the questions might be appropriate for future sessions. You may also think of your own. It's usually a good idea to end the questioning session when the group energy is high, with a feeling that more could be explored.

✭ I wonder which part of this story you liked best…

✭ I wonder which part you thought was the most important…

✭ I wonder if there is any part of this story that you would like to leave out…

✭ I wonder how you felt during the different parts of the story…

✭ I wonder if there are any other parts of this story that need to be included…

✭ I wonder what might happen if we change the order of things in this story…

✭ I wonder if these things… *(point to the Easter story objects)*… could be anything else…

✭ I wonder what would happen to this story if we added the 'bump in the night' objects… *(point to the boxes and bags)*

✭ I wonder if there is anything from the other stories that we have heard that we could bring to this story…*(It would be helpful to have the other artefacts from the previous sessions on display in the room)*

✭ I wonder what we might do with all the stories we have heard…

✭ I wonder what we might really do about the things that go bump in the night…

Closing this part of the session

When you feel that the energy has gone out of the discussion, you will need to find some way of showing that this part of the session is ending and the next is about to begin. One way is to bring people's attention to the materials.

A simple gesture of the hand can do this, with some simple closing remark or some affirmation about the quality of response. It may be that you suggest a moment of silence to reflect on what has been said. Then move on to give instructions for the next part of your process.

If you decide to put the materials away at this point, turn to page 16 for some suggestions as to how this might be done.

Either at this point or at the very end, when all the materials have been gathered together and replaced into their containers and baskets, you could lay your hands on the materials and say…

God looked at the world and loved it so much…

APPENDIX ONE

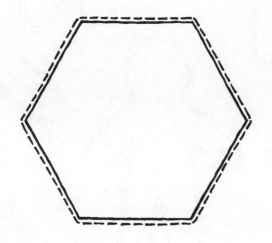

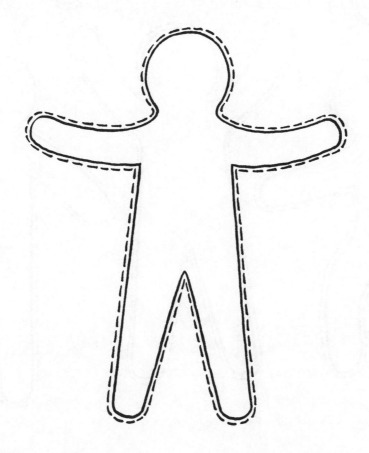

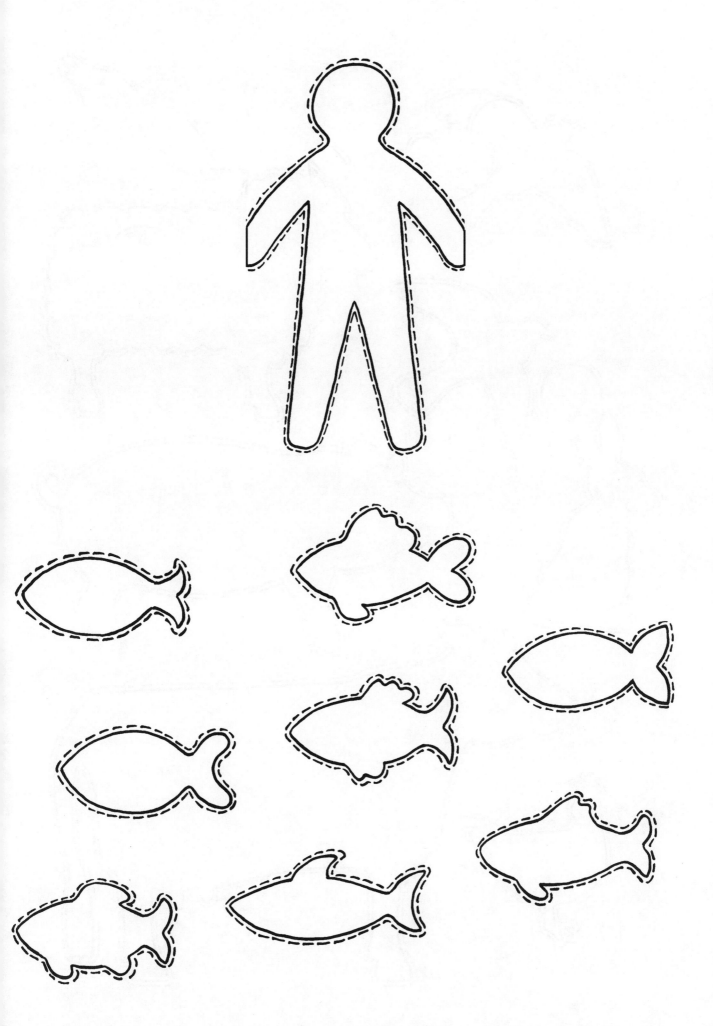

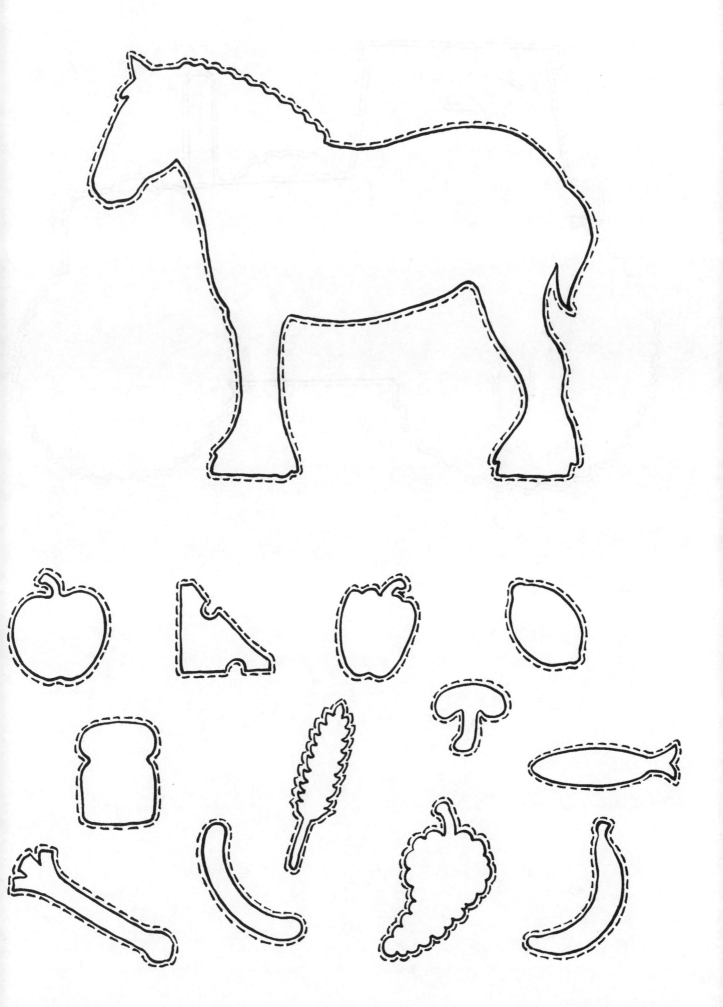

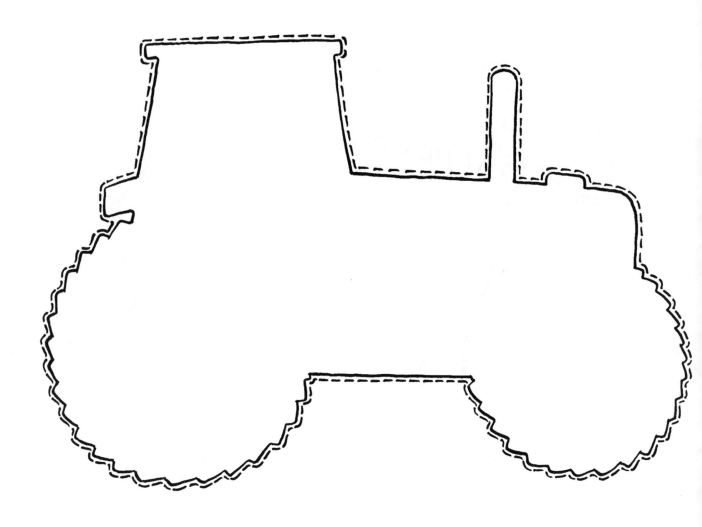

Reproduced with permission from *Living in a fragile world* published by BRF 2003 (1 84101 325 0)

APPENDIX TWO

Below are some alternative exercises for use during the creative activity time. Although these activities may be used for any of the sessions, they are particularly suited to the sessions indicated.

Take a line for a walk

This exercise is particularly suited to Session One.

Provide a large piece of paper, big enough for the whole group to work on. You may have to glue several sheets together. Have available a wide range of oil pastels, which have rich and deep colours (crayons are a second best). Each person chooses one or two of the pastels, their favourite colours. They then draw meandering lines across the paper, taking their lines for a walk. Where the lines intersect, irregular spaces are created. Using a wide variety of coloured pastels, each of the sections and spaces can then be filled with graffiti, blocks of colour, patterns, symbols, or images that represent different parts of the experience. People can be encouraged to change the colours between different sections. At the end of the exercise, a very light wash of a water-based paint applied with broad brushes adds another dimension: the wax of the pastels resists the water. (Keep the paint thin and watery.)

Someone leads the group, offering different suggestions, such as: 'Fill in a space that represents... *your feelings during the last thirty minutes... your hopes... something you would like to say... an image that has stayed in your mind... something that you would like to question... the part you would like to leave out*' and so on.

Once you get going, different members of the group may well come up with suggestions for ways to fill in the spaces. This exercise can also be done individually on a smaller scale with a sheet of A4 paper. At the end, you may want to spend some time offering people an opportunity to express any new insights, confirmation of thoughts, new questions and so on.

Creative collaging

This exercise is particularly suited to Session Two.

You will need:
- ☆ Scraps of coloured paper *(include a wide variety of textures and colours)*
- ☆ Gold and silver foil
- ☆ Card
- ☆ Tissue
- ☆ Crêpe paper
- ☆ Newspaper (the greater the variety, the better)
- ☆ Some small sheets of coloured plain paper
- ☆ Oil pastels
- ☆ Coloured felts and scraps of fabric
- ☆ Some larger sheets of coloured sugar paper
- ☆ Glue
- ☆ Scissors

Invite the participants to respond to the discussion or story in the following way.

Use the larger sheets of paper as the broad landscape. Cut, colour and stick the smaller scraps to create symbols to represent the elements and the contents of the landscape.

Landscape can be understood in any way—geographical, spiritual, inner/outer, emotional and so on.

Allow people an opportunity to give voice to their thoughts if they wish. Others may want to present their piece without words.

Family role play

This exercise is particularly suited to Session Three.

> **You will need:**
> ★ A selection of homemade cards (at least one card for every member of the group), with the name of a member of an imaginary family. This could be a nuclear family or, using a wider understanding, the world family. Each card needs to contain a short description of the person, and a story outlining their circumstances.

The cards can be prepared in advance, or the group members could prepare them together at the beginning of the session. If the latter option is adopted, during the exercise it is not necessary for the group members to work with the card they have personally prepared.

Each participant is invited to choose a card and asked to think about what feelings this person has. What relationship might they have with other members of the family?

Imagine that the family is gathered together. Ask the question, 'If the centre of the room is the place where you might feel most comfortable and included, where might you place yourself in the room?'

Each person then has an opportunity to say how it feels, being in the place they are.

Each person has an opportunity to speak to another member of the family—to ask questions and so on.

It is very important to debrief this exercise and to allow each person in the group to come out of his or her imagined role.